MINI MEDITATIONS ON

JOY

Adam & Lisa Murphy

LIMINAL 11

First published in 2018 by Liminal 11

Illustrated by Adam Murphy
Coloured by Lisa Murphy

Book design by Mike Medaglia

Printed in Slovenia

ISBN 978-1-912634-02-6

10 9 8 7 6 5 4 3 2 1

www.liminal11.com

MINI MEDITATIONS ON

JOY

Adam & Lisa Murphy

INTRODUCTIONS

When (series editor, awesome artist and good friend) Mike Medaglia approached us about doing a book of quotes, we both knew we would say yes.

But then I heard the topic — can you illustrate 48 quotes on Joy? Um, sure, I can do that. No problem. But my heart sank a little. How do I tell people about joy when I'm mired in the middle of a massive depression; stressed, angry, tired, not very joyful at all? And especially when my life is actually filled with things to be joyful about, and it's me and my terrible attitude that's preventing me from seeing them? What kind of hypocrite spends a whole book inciting people to find their joy when he's failing so spectacularly to do so himself?

The universe has had a way of sending what I need, not what I think I need. And what I'm ready for, not what I think I'm ready for. That's how I met Lisa. And as Mike wisely said, sometimes quotes go in and bury themselves, only to germinate later. Or something like that; I suspect his version was more eloquent.

Anyway, so it proved. This book has been a wonderful and often surprising vehicle for my own re-discovery of that radiant, unceasing, everyday sort of joy that I suspect is buried somewhere deep in the core of all of us. It's so easy to lose track of, but it's always there, waiting patiently.

May you find your way back to your own joy. And if this book can help in any way, I'll be very glad.

Alan Murphy

I was delighted when Mike asked for me to colour this book. Joy is something that has always called to me. Look! Look at the steam rising from a cup. Crunch that ice cube! The smell of freshly cleaned sheets. I guess you can say I experience joy in the mundane, the ordinary, the uncelebrated. And I found this project en-JOY-able. Hee hee :)

Lisa C. K. Murphy

make PEACE with the Universe.
TAKE joy iN it.
It will TurN to Gold.
-Rumi

The pleasantest things in the world are: PLEASANT Thoughts: and the great ART of Life is to have as MANY of them as POSSIBLE.

- Michel de Montaigne

Joy
does not
simply
happen
to us.
We have to
choose
joy
and keep
choosing it
every
day.

— Henri Nouwen

Ever since happiness
heard your name,

It has been

running

through

the

streets

trying to find you.
- Hafez

we are FRAGILE CREATURES and it is from this WEAKNESS, not despite it, that we DISCOVER the possibility of TRUE JOY.

-DESMOND TUTU

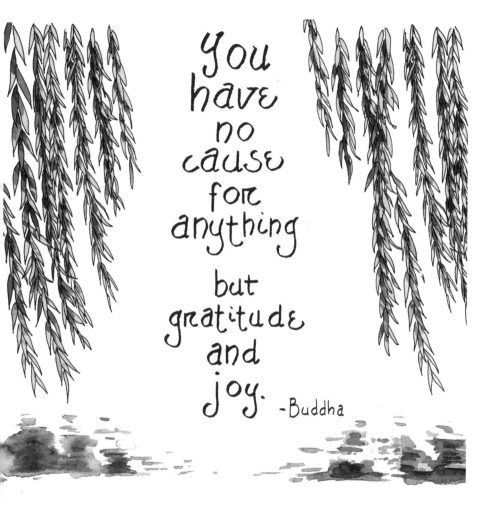

YOU have to sniff out Joy. Keep your Nose to THE JOY TRAIL.
-BuffY SAInte-MariE

I'm not afraid of Storms, for I'm Learning how to Sail my Ship.

— Louisa May Alcott

It is only possible to live

happily ever after

on a day-to-day basis.

— Margaret Bonanno

Joy is as thorny and sharp
as any of the
dark emotions.
To love someone fiercely,
to believe in something
with your whole heart,
to celebrate a
fleeting moment in time,
to fully engage in a life
that doesn't come
with guarantees –
these are the risks that involve
vulnerability
and often pain.

-Brené Brown

There's just no accounting for happiness or the way it turns up like a prodigal who comes back to the dust at your feet having squandered a fortune far away.

~Jane Kenyon

Once we recognise what it is we are feeling,
Once we recognise we can
love deeply, feel deeply,
can feel joy,
then we will demand that
ALL parts of our lives
produce that kind
of joy.
- Audre Lorde

All your pain,
worry,
sorrow,

will someday
apologise
and confess

they were
a *great lie.*

-Hafez

People from a planet without **flowers**
would think we must be
mad with joy the whole time
to have such things
around us.
–Iris Murdoch

JOY IS WHAT happens TO US
    WHEN WE allow OURSELVES TO Recognise
        how good THINGS REALLY ARE.

-MARIANNE WILLIAMSON

Joy! Joy! I triumph!
Now no more I know
          Myself as simply ME.   -Attar

Know that joy
is rarer,
more difficult,
and more beautiful
than sadness.

Once you make this
all-important discovery,
you must
embrace
joy
as a
moral obligation.

— andré gide

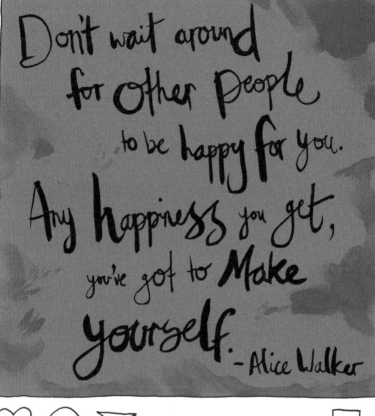

Sometimes your joy is the source of your smile,
but sometimes your smile is the source of your joy.

-Thich Nhat Hanh

From the VERY CORE of our BEING
we simply desire JOY & CONTENTMENT.

But so often THESE FEELINGS ARE HARD to FIND,
like a BUTTERFLY
that LANDS on us

and then FLUTTERS AWAY.

-Dalai Lama XIV

Whenever you are creating beauty around you,

you
 are
  restoring
   your
    own
     soul.

-Alice Walker

What
shall I call
thee?

" I
happy
am.

Joy
is my
name, – "

Sweet joy
befall
thee!

–William Blake

A
thing
of beauty
is a
joy
forever.

— John Keats

I am still learning –
    how to take joy in all the people I am,
        how to use all my selves in the service of what I believe,
        how to accept when I fail
            and rejoice when I succeed.

                    – Audre Lorde

If I keep
  a green bough
    in my heart,

  the
    singing bird
      will come.

  ~ Chinese Proverb

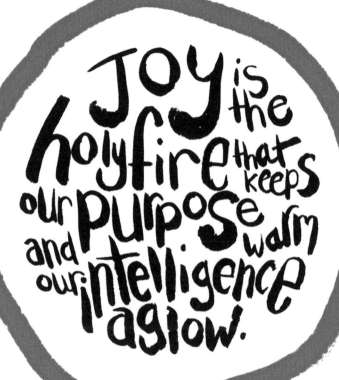

JOY is the holyfire that keeps our purpose warm and our intelligence aglow.

—Helen Keller

Some things are little on the outside,
and rough and common,
but I remember the time
when the dust of the streets
were as pleasing as Gold
to my infant eyes.

-Thomas
Traherne

Now and then
it's good to pause
in our pursuit of happiness

and just be happy.

- Guilliame Apollinaire

It's the great mystery of human life that old grief passes gradually into quiet tender joy.

- Fyodor Dostoevsky

There is not one blade of grass,
there is
no colour in this world
that is not intended
to make us

Rejoice.

— John Calvin

Those who wish to Sing always find a Song

— Swedish Proverb

Joy is portable.
Take it with you.
                                    -Anon.

You have to participate relentlessly in the manifestations of your own blessings.

-Elizabeth Gilbert

Happiness is not a goal, it is a by-product of a life well lived.

—Eleanor Roosevelt

Also in the Mini Meditations series:

Designed for the creative soul and those that
aspire to be, *Mini Meditations on Creativity* is
an inspirational gem.

ISBN: 978-1-912634-01-9

light at the **crossroads**